The Groom's Secret Handbook

How Not to Screw Up the Biggest Day of Her Life

Anthony E. Marsh and Jay Blumenfield

A Fireside Book
Published by Simon & Schuster

To Anne,
You are the love of my life
(even though you didn't let me
pick the dinnerware)

To the future Mrs. B.,
May you be well stacked

F FIRESIDE
Rockefeller Center
1230 Avenue of the Americas
New York, NY 10020

Designed by Bonni Leon-Berman

Manufactured in the United States of America

1 3 5 7 9 10 8 6 4 2

Library of Congress Cataloging-in-Publication Data
Marsh, Anthony E.
The groom's secret handbook : how not to screw up the biggest day
of her life / Anthony E. Marsh and Jay Blumenfield.
     p.   cm.
     1. Marriage—Humor.   I. Blumenfield, Jay.   II. Title.
PN6231.M3M36 1997   97-20077
818'.5407—dc21   CIP
ISBN 0-684-83316-6

Contents

Consider This, Buddy
An Introduction

All that a recently engaged guy must do to get a glimpse of his future is open the dictionary and find that the word "groom" is defined as "a man or boy employed to take care of horses." And although women will argue that the proper term for a marrying man is "bridegroom," the message should be clear. For a groom, a wedding is no party. A wedding is something that happens *to* him, not for him. A wedding is the culmination of a rigorous planning regimen in which he may have about as much say as a feed bag.

We created this book as a much needed tonic for all men in this unique position. During the wedding process, a groom cannot help but be inundated by a torrent of frustration. Like good electroshock therapy, each chapter is designed to dissuade him from potential wrong moves, from slips of the tongue that can get him buried under an avalanche of animosity and sexless evenings. But remember, having nothing to say is the worst error of all. It is critical that a groom maintain an opinion because his budding bride always needs something to talk him out of.

As veterans of the wedding wars, we feel confident that this book contains all the information necessary to get an altar-bound guy through the problem spots, over the hurdles, and out from the shadows of his own stupidity. We are not responsible, however, in any way for the outcome (unless positive) of a particular wedding, relationship, or life. Because let's face facts, in today's times getting married is like being ridden hard and put away wet. Call it divine retribution or karmic justice, just don't call it a joke and throw this book away. If a groom takes these sentiments to heart, maybe, just maybe, he'll keep what little sanity he has left and make it to the honeymoon happy, healthy, and still loved.

Chapter One

The Engagement

Rockin' and Kneelin'

The Girlfriend

Getting married is one of the most fantastic things in the world, ranking right up there with winning concert tickets on the radio and getting your parents to lend you their house for the weekend. Yet unlike the latter, marriage has rules. And when it comes to deciding if you have made the right decision, these rules should not be taken lightly. In order to live a happy-ever-after existence, you must pay attention to certain warning signs in your soon-to-be legally committed relationship. Otherwise you may wind up the brunt of everyone's cruel jokes—that is, more than you usually are.

So before it's too late, take the following quiz and find out . . .

Is Your Girl a Blood-Sucking Leech?

(Because if she is, it's time you had her lanced.)

Answer *honestly* and select the response that best applies to your situation.

1. You have started to lose touch with
    a. your friends
    b. yourself (if you know what we mean)
    c. your bank account
2. Have you ever seen her
    a. going through your refrigerator
    b. going through your sock drawer
    c. going through your wallet and removing all your cash
3. Do you find yourself suddenly enjoying activities like
    a. moonlit walks and picnics in the park
    b. napping
    c. working her part-time job for her

4. Do her nicknames for you resemble
   a. sweetie
   b. pookie-wookie
   c. pudgy-balding-time-consumer

5. Does she try to influence your taste in
   a. movies
   b. food
   c. other guys for her to date

6. Have you seen an image of her
   a. in your dreams
   b. in a friend's yearbook
   c. on *America's Most Wanted*

7. After going out, have you ever heard her go to the phone and call
   a. her mother
   b. her clergyman
   c. her bookie

8. She occasionally points out
   a. the places she used to live a kid
   b. the places she used to play as a kid
   c. the place she lives with her other husband and kids

9. She encourages you to share the same
   a. interests
   b. underwear
   c. credit cards

10. You've begun to overlook slight human flaws that have bothered you in the past like
    a. an odd laugh or birthmark
    b. the fact that she's really into sports
    c. the fact that she's sixty-five, doesn't speak a word of English, and is dating you only to get legal citizenship

11. After making out, you find yourself wishing she would
    a. cuddle with you longer
    b. whisper sweet nothings
    c. remember your name

Scoring: All answers of (a) score one point, answers of (b) score two points, and answers of (c) score three points, with an exception on question 9 where the answer (b) requires that you call the *Montel Williams Show*. They'll explain.

11 points: This means you have the type of relationship the author of this quiz deems "normal" and "healthy." You make a fine couple and we wish you the best of luck. (Of course, the authors of this quiz often stay up real late for no reason and eat Ding-Dongs and Pretzel-Cheese Combos until they're too sick to move.)

12-22 points: This means you have a fine relationship. Your girlfriend is still worth marrying, though the higher the score, the more you should consider hiring a private investigator to shadow her every move just to be sure.

23-32 points: Scrap the loser. She's dead weight. You can do better. If your score tops the 30 mark, you could probably do better joining a pen pal to an inmate program.

33 points: Drop your pen and run. Run fast.

The Ring

So you've passed the quiz, or maybe you just don't give a damn. Either way, you're ready to be married and there's no stopping you. It's time to pop the question. You just need a ring and you're all set. Now simply march down to your bank and withdraw your life's savings, then borrow some more from your folks, maybe a little from your friends, then hock your car, take a loan, and sell a kidney or two. Hey, what's schlepping around a dialysis machine when it comes to showing your woman how much you want to be together for all eternity? Because nothing says commitment to a woman like a rock that comes from South African soil and sets you back three months' salary.

Up until this moment, you have probably never given this particular rock much thought. Ironic, isn't it? The item you are about to spend more money on than you ever thought could be spent in one place for something that you can't drive is an item you know nothing about. And the real irony is that your woman does know all there is to know. In fact, she has known all about the "4 C's of Diamonds"—carat, cut, clarity, and color—since childhood. Think back to elementary school. Remember when they would separate the boys and girls, and you would be shown a film by the gym teacher about car wrecks. Well, the girls were getting the diamond-ring movies.

Unfortunately, you can't ask your future fiancée to give you the skinny, because this is supposed to be a surprise. You must contact everyone you know with connections to the diamond industry. (Surprisingly, you'll find that everyone, including the kid who bags your groceries, knows someone who can't wait to give you "the deal of a lifetime.") Take all that information, mull it over awhile, and make the most informed selection you can, understanding that you are going to get screwed regardless. Let's face facts: a diamond is nothing more than an overdigested piece of coal—the kidney stone of earth's urinary tract. If you have done your homework correctly, the following true-or-false challenge will be a breeze.

The Jeweler Challenge

Respond true or false to the following statements:

- A good jeweler should allow you to fondle his stones.
  Answer: True. But only if he's wearing pants.

- A good jeweler should explain "clarity" as the measure of a stone's imperfections.
  Answer: True. Clarity is not the measure of your imperfection as a person spending up to a year's salary on a rock.

- A good jeweler believes "the bigger the table, the better the ring looks."
  Answer: False. That guy also believes "the bigger the cushion, the better the pushin'."

- A good jeweler should deal "Wholesale to the Public."
  Answer: False. "Wholesale to the Public" is as big an oxymoron as "marital bliss."

- A good jeweler should hum "Diamonds Are a Girl's Best Friend" while serving you.
  Answer: True. Especially if said jeweler wants his tongue ripped out and engraved with your wedding date.

- A good jeweler should know that zirconium is Latin for "cheap bastard."
  Answer: False. He should know that it's Latin for "I'm dumping you for a guy with real money."

- A good jeweler should advise you that white gold looks exactly like platinum.
  Answer: True. But a *great* jeweler will tell your fiancée that it *is* platinum.

The Proposal

It seems like a pretty basic concept. You ask, she answers. You've done it a million times. Want to go to the movies? Yeah, sure. How 'bout dinner? Great, I'm famished. Wanna get down on all fours and bark like a dog for me? Sure, I'll be there in a sec.

Although it may appear simple, this particular question is probably the most loaded one you will ever ask. Think about it this way: Her friends never inquire, "How did he ask you to the movies? Was it raining? Was he nervous?" *This* particular question *will* live on in legend. Your beloved will tell the story of your proposal for the rest of time—at family get-togethers, at dinners with PTA friends, and to complete strangers—whenever the mood may strike. So you better make it extra special. But whatever you do or say, stay away from these particular openers. Trust us, we know.

Proposals One Should Not Utter—Ever

- "I think you are probably as good as I am going to get, so uh, I guess we should get married."

- "I am incredibly afraid of becoming a lonely bald old man, so marry me now . . . please."
- "Well, I guess now that your cute sister is taken, I'll have to settle for you."
- "Look, I just don't have enough money to date anymore."
- "My parents will pay you generously for your troubles."
- "If you don't marry me, the government will deport me and I will be beheaded by the Hezbollah."
- "Will you please stay home and raise my children, keep my house, and stand by my side while I go out and boink every bimbo from here to Malta?"
- "Uh, could you help me up, I think my back just went out."
- "Do you know how much money we could save in tax incentives if we got hitched?"
- "Will you emotionally and legally bind yourself and your finances to me for the rest of your life or at whatever point you decide to give me half."
- "Would you marry me so that we can each have sex with the same person over and over and over and over for years upon years, never tasting the pleasure of new flesh, never again feeling the flush of unknown lips and untouched passions, just the same person again and again and again until it is as exciting as taking a dump."
- "Look, if it doesn't work out we can always get a divorce."
- "Without a wedding nobody gets any cool presents . . . so let's get married, okay?"

(Note: As for the proposals to utter, we figure anything not covered here is fair game. Good luck now and try not to break wind when you drop to one knee.)

Comparing the Ring

Remember those fun-filled days spent cavorting naked around the high school locker room? All that macho braggadocio, those exotic strains of foot fungus, and, of course, the shower-stall swordfights.

Well, now that you've forgone the hassle of consuming food in favor of the rock on your loved one's finger, prepare yourself for the treacherous trip down memory lane. The engagement ring is in its essence much like a teeny locker room. It carries the constant reminder that while tales of quality do count, size reigns supreme. That's why it's important to draw upon the lessons of your youth and help embellish the description of the ring, while not belittling the opposing machinery too much. Just as you would refrain from asking the water polo team about steroid-induced impotence, you should try to avoid remarks that get you stuffed head first into a toilet. Here are the types of comments you should shun when the inevitable comparisons are made of your fiancée's engagement ring to another:

What Not to Say about Another Woman's Ring

- "I'll bet that ring fetches a pretty penny when you guys break up."
- "Forget 'color, clarity, cut, and carat size,' your ring has chutzpah."
- "Hope that mugger's beacon doesn't put you in any danger in this city."

- "Did you guys get two tickets to a Wayne Newton concert with that?"
- "It might be small, but our diamond was mined by Mr. DeBeers personally."
- "Maybe I shouldn't say anything, but I can see the faint image of Sy Sperling in yours."
- "I actually gave the other half of my budget to a homeless shelter."
- "I'm just glad my wife's not taking the risk of getting carpal tunnel syndrome."
- "It's not the size of the prize, but the motion of the ocean."
- "You guys still think you'll get into Heaven?"
- "That's a lovely stone (cough, cough). Gold digger (cough, cough)."
- "That rock looks fabulous on you. If you only had a turban and a pack of Tarot cards you could make some pocket change down at the boardwalk."
- "I'm guessing that thing tears the hell out of the sheets at night. I mean, that's assuming you still get any."
- "I guess your kids won't be needing college."
- "I opted for the smaller investment. All my money's tied up in cash."
- "I bet you still sting from the colossal screwing you took on that bad boy."

Meeting the In-Laws

The girl of your dreams has said yes and the whirlwind has begun. But although she wants to spend the rest of her life with you, you are not home free just yet. There are still some people you have to pass muster with. Yes . . . the IN-LAWS. You cannot have any sort of misery-free existence without first impressing the two people who are responsible for your fiancée's existence.

Now, don't be nervous when you first meet them. Just because your every move will be scrutinized with the precision of a famished hyena on its first kill in over a month, and your every utterance will be held against you for the next fifty years, winning over her parents need not be a problem. Follow the tips given here and they will be calling you their prodigal son in no time. Of course, they will also be calling you at home at any time, so don't make 'em love you too much, if you know what we mean.

To make the best impression on your future in-laws, you have to size them up first. If you know who you're dealing with, it will be easier to tailor your personality and make them fall for you like a Valujet over the Everglades. Remember, this is not about being yourself. It is about figuring out who these people are and making them love you more than their own daughter. You will have only a split second before you must switch on the appropriate personality. If you memorize the following greeting/personality analysis in-law chart, you will be well equipped to manipulate their affections.

The Father's Greeting

A knuckle-crunching handshake

A hug

A high-five

A two-handed shake

A weak, wet, clammy shake

The ol' fake-shake-to-the-rub-of-the-hair bit

No shake, no nothing

Kisses on both cheeks

The side arm thumb shake

A military salute

The Analysis

He's self-conscious about his toupee.

He's bisexual.

He will, at some point, make you listen to his bootleg Dead tapes.

He's packing heat.

Opportunity exists for hostile takeover of his bank account.

He will soon ask you to pull his finger.

A little man in his head won't stop yelling, "You're fucking my daughter, you're fucking my daughter."

He doesn't shower, and he has a mistress.

He had better have a rotator-cuff injury.

He's a retired officer or a recent escapee from a sanitarium. (Either way, salute back. He can kill you with his bare hands.)

The Mother's Greeting

A kiss on the cheek

An extended hand

A prepared drink

A high-five

An air-kiss

A hug

A wave

A slap on the back

A slam of a door and a scream of, "My daughter is not getting married to this loser!"

The Analysis

She secretly desires you.

She secretly desires you.

She secretly desires you.

She secretly desires you.

She secretly desires you.

She secretly desires you.

She secretly desires you.

She secretly desires you.

She secretly desires you.

Chatting Up the In-Laws

You have read the chart and you know who you are dealing with. Now it's time to let the conversation fly. It won't be half as bad as you imagined. Remember, they're parents. They love to talk about the good old days when families kept their secrets in the closet and "crack" was only that space between your butt cheeks. Keep in mind that they also love to hear big-time promises of all the things you'll buy for them someday. Forget talking about making their daughter happy; go for the glory and mention your dream of whisking them away for a year on your tropical island, replete with drivers, cooks, and occasional pantry raids by Brando. Sit back, relax, and enjoy the gabfest. Just don't stumble out of the blocks by saying any of the following major faux pas.

Things Not to Say to Her Parents

- "Do you want to be called Mommie or Momma?"
- "Don't think of it as losing a daughter, think of it as gaining a tax write-off."
- "When can we discuss how I'd like my room decorated?"
- "Can I borrow the car?"
- "I'll bet the anticipation and excitement of the wedding night was a lot greater in your day."
- "You guys are still going to give us a wedding present, aren't you?"
- "Have I shown you the body pierce I got for this glorious occasion?"
- "Did you guys invite those policemen?"
- "As good looking as your daughter is, some of her friends are really babes."
- "This is going to be the best wedding I've had, so far."
- "God, I hate children, don't you?"
- "I think the little missus would look good smoking a stogie."
- "Hey, Pops, is jock itch contagious?"
- "Damn, you guys probably have some ugly relatives."
- "When's the boozin' begin?"
- "I really hope my folks don't vomit at this one."
- "I like my scotch like I like my women . . . aged in the basement and about fifteen years old."

THE FRIENDS OF

AMY LYNN RICHMOND

request your presence

at an engagement party,

because after threatening to leave him

high and dry, bloated and toothless

alone in a dingy apartment

overlooking a refinery,

Joe Camposola

finally got off the pot

and popped the question

Dealing with Married People

Advice Versa: A One-Act Play

Setting: Overpriced dinner spot

Characters: Your fiancée's friends and their obnoxious husbands

Time: When you least want it to occur

YOU: Hi, everyone. Nice to meet you.

BOOMER *(the former football-playing husband of your fiancée's best friend):* Nice to meet you? Whaddaya talking about little man . . . *(giving you a harder than needed slap on the back).* Welcome to the club.

YOU *(gasping for air):* Club? What club?

CHAD *(blond hunk who married your fiancée's sister):* The married men's club, my new friend. Say good-bye to your single pals, we men who have given up our freedom have to stick together.

BOOMER: You can't fool around anymore . . . at least not in the open *(guffaw, guffaw).* Although with your woman, I don't suppose you'll want to . . . not for the first six months, that is. *(Elbow in your side, laughter all around.)*

YOU *(uncomfortable chuckle and glance at your woman, who's engrossed in ring discussions at the other end of the table)*: Um, uhh . . .

CHAD: Listen, brother . . . I guess I can call you that now, huh Broskeee? You know I always wanted to be with two sisters, maybe after the honeymoon we can do a swap-a-roony. *(wink, wink)* You know what they say about incest being best?

YOU *(calling out)*: Scotch and soda, please.

BOOMER: Scooter, don't mind him, he's just ribbing you. But seriously now, have you been giving thought to your centerpiece plans. A centerpiece can make or break a wedding.

TYLER *(with more hair gel than hair)*: Wrong. Food is the key. You like food, don't you?

YOU: Of course, who doesn't.

TYLER *(firing an invisible gun at you)*: Implement a good seabass. People love a good sea-bass. *(All nod in agreement.)*

WAYLON *(mustachioed and overcologned)*: Son, I have what my friends like to call a perfect marriage, and do you know why I have a perfect marriage?

YOU *(downing drink)*: Because your wife's not old enough to press charges?

WAYLON: I have a perfect marriage because I took my sweet lady on the perfect honeymoon. Do you know where I took her, son?

YOU: To the other end of the trailer park?

WAYLON: I took her to Branson, Missouri. They got these

wild hoedown clubs all in a row there. We almost didn't come home, son.

YOU: Stop calling me son. I think I'm older than you.

CHAD: Bro, chill out. All he's trying to say is that all you have to worry about is how the band leader is dressed. If you make sure that the guy leading your wedding band is wearing the right stuff, you're home free.

YOUR FIANCÉE *(arriving just in the nick of time)*: Sweetie, we've just been invited to a barbecue this weekend. All of these guys will be there. Isn't it great?

YOU: Scratch the south of France, we're going to Branson!

Fight Break

Things might be going along peacefully, but it takes just one, small flippant response to cause a full-blown Armageddon.

Fight Topic: Changing Last Names

YOUR FIANCÉE: Why should I be the one that changes my last name?

YOU: Because I'm the man, and that's the way it's always been.

YOUR FIANCÉE: Well, I happen to be quite fond of my last name.

YOU: So was Manson.

YOUR FIANCÉE: Are you saying that my family name reminds you of a murderer's?

YOU: You're missing the point.

YOUR FIANCÉE: And how do you know Manson was his mother's maiden name?

YOU: Sorry. I could have simply said, "A rose is a rose by any other name."

YOUR FIANCÉE: Oh, like now quoting Shakespeare is going to make me swoon and be all forgiving?

YOU: Uh . . .

YOUR FIANCÉE: Forget it. Changing my name is like cutting off a limb.

YOU: Is your tongue considered a limb?

YOUR FIANCÉE: If you think this is a silly matter, we can call off the whole wedding, right here.

YOU: Maybe I should change my last name instead.

YOUR FIANCÉE: It's sure time that some men did.

YOU: Yeah, I'll change it to "Argued-to-death."

YOUR FIANCÉE: Real cute. We'll see who laughing last.

YOU: It'll be a tie between the caterer and the florist.

YOUR FIANCÉE: What's that crack supposed to mean?

YOU: That the photographer's *only* charging us three times too much.

YOUR FIANCÉE: I'm calling my mother.

YOU: By her maiden name, I hope.

Panic

The fight has triggered a synaptical brain explosion. Your heart begins to race, your eyes blur, sweat begins to shoot from your every pore. You're too young for a heart attack, and you're not even close to your parents' house. What is happening to you? All of a sudden and for no reason, you remember an old girlfriend. You think of her naked. The little man in your head begins to yell through his megaphone.

THIS IS IT, PAL. THE ONLY BIG MILESTONE LEFT IS DEATH. YOU WILL NEVER HAVE SEX WITH ANOTHER WOMAN AGAIN WITHOUT COMMITTING ADULTERY. GET OUT NOW, WHILE YOU STILL CAN. WHILE YOU STILL CAN HAVE ANOTHER MENAGE À TROIS. ANOTHER? WHO ARE YOU KIDDING? YOU NEVER EVEN HAD ONE. THIS IS THE END. YOU'LL NEVER HAVE SEX WITH PAMELA ANDERSON OR RACQUEL WELCH OR HER DAUGHTER. NEVER.

This is called a *panic attack*. Do not call your doctor. It happens to all prospective grooms, and it happens often, sometimes striking without warning. There are but two known methods that effectively stop the little man with the megaphone dead in his tracks. Following either of these treatments will get you back on the path to an easy wedding in no time.

Method 1: Self Depreciation

Step 1: Look at yourself in the mirror.

Step 2: Repeat the words, "Why would anyone want to marry this guy, let alone a babe like my fiancée?"

Step 3: Hone in on your worst feature. Are you going bald? Are you developing a gut? Are you beginning to gray at the temples? Is hair starting to sprout from your earlobes?

Step 4: Close your eyes, and pretend you are a computer morphing machine like they used in the *Terminator* or those razor commercials. Now picture your worst feature as it gets worse through the years. How much hair is growing out of your earlobes? In five years, ten, twenty-five? Not a pretty picture, is it? It's not gonna be too easy to get a mate looking like that, is it?

Method 2: The Past Wasn't That Great

Step 1: Sit down.

Step 2: Picture that ex-girlfriend who just drifted into your mind. The one you think you need to be naked with immediately.

Step 3: Now calmly think back to the last days of your relationship with her. You were disgusted with her. The way she chewed her food. You hated those Swedish art films she would drag you to, except for that one about the au pair sisters coming to terms with their lesbianism. You hated her friends. But the sex was pretty good, you tell yourself. But was it?

Step 4: Think back. Really think back. Remember the way she slurped her cereal, never laughed at your best jokes, talked too much in the movies. Oh yeah, and remember when she told all her friends about how you weep openly every time you make a good bowel movement.

Step 5: Remind yourself that you were sick of her and you would be again.

Chapter Two

The Planning

Devise and Conquer

The Location

The chapel is in foreclosure, the hotel banquet hall is booked indefinitely, and your parents' backyard can only seat fourteen people and a cat. What do you do? As you will come to realize, there are way too many factors that go into the decision of location. So before you rent out the balcony at the XXX theater down the block, play our little board game.

The Location Game

Directions: You and your fiancée each take a turn rolling a die. Advance the appropriate number of spaces, following the directions described for that square. Continue until one person comes to a decision or the die is hurled across the room and permanently embedded in the wall.

1. Aunt Edna is still hooked up to life support, wedding must be close to home, roll again.

2. Fiancée's family is sued by a disgruntled cable guy, no money for fancy location, roll again.

3. Half your family is wiped out in a freak Tyco-racing accident, extra funds now available, move ahead three spaces.

4. Decide to get married on a Carnival cruise, forget that you will be hounded by a shnockered Kathy Lee Gifford and a fun-lovin' strain of salmonella, lose turn.

5. Elope to Las Vegas, gamble away nest egg during vows, go back three spaces and roll again using a weighted die.

6. Plan to have ceremony in San Antonio, inadvertently forget the Alamo, go back four spaces.

7. Rob bank to pay for "open bar," go to jail, do not collect bride.

8. Book Yankee Stadium, overlook potential that "rice throwing" will become "free mini–baseball bat throwing," lose consciousness and turn.

9. Receive and accept mail-offer "Fantasy Island Wedding," go forward four spaces.

 10. Plan to marry on the space shuttle, lose twenty years preparing to become an astronaut, go back to dating circuit.

 11. Learn that your wedding night falls on February 29, leap forward one space.

 12. Minister secretly marries you during a conference with him, lose your religion and roll again.

 13. Learn that island's only inhabitant is the ghost of Herve Villachaize, go back one space.

 14. Plan wedding on floor of New York Stock Exchange, make ten grand on pork futures, lose thirty on some Internet company, go back four spaces.

 15. Get sideswiped by a police car, collect settlement, move ahead three spaces.

 16. Win the lottery, float through life, no need ever to roll again.

17. Plan wedding on North Pole to be "on top of the world," cold feet become gangrenous, go back two spaces.

18. Book Sistine Chapel and fly guests to Rome.

19. Get married on the Concorde; guests joining mile-high club at Mach 1 sue for various injuries, go back five spaces.

20. Hold ceremony on the Eiffel Tower overlooking the romantic City of Lights or tie the knot in rush hour traffic holding a baguette, just put an end to this merciless game.

21. Threaten to blow up desirable hotel unless they remove charge for folding each chair, apologize, and go back one space.

22. Book fiancée's dream location on the perfect day for the perfect price (*Note*: This space on the board does not exist).

The Gifts

There are some positive, long-lasting rewards that come out of all this wedding planning . . . presents and lots of 'em. Plus, in one of the great twists of etiquette, when it comes to weddings, you are *supposed* to tell people what to give you. It's not considered tacky at all to direct people to a list of exactly what you want, complete with prices.

This crazy process is called "registering" and, if you want to come away from your big day like you just won both showcases on *The Price Is Right*, it is a necessity. This means, however, that you must register at the proper establishments. You must not go with your first instinct of registering at Bank of America or the Anheuser-Busch factory outlet.

The actual process is grueling. You will be dragged on an

invisible leash from store to store, unable to walk past even the simplest of items. You will be inundated with details about household articles you never knew existed, let alone needed. And, of course, you will become depleted of the energy required to stifle comments about the hairy mole on the saleswoman's chin or the greedy glint in your fiancée's eye. Dip into your reserve tanks, keeping in mind that long after your love is gone, sterling place settings are still valuable, and refrain from saying any of the following comments.

Things Not to Say While Registering for Gifts

- "Doesn't this store have china with little section dividers for your mashed potatoes?"
- "What? We need more than one set of sheets?"
- "Personally, I think wine tastes better straight from the bottle."
- "Like hell we don't need an extra radio-controlled dune buggy."
- "Sure, but aren't plastic utensils just as functional?"
- "Make sure it's made of something that won't shatter when I'm in one of my *moods*."
- "You pick it. I don't plan on setting foot in the kitchen."
- "Let's skip the formal stuff. Nobody's coming for dinner if you're cooking."
- "That Italian silver probably melts down better, huh?"
- "Select a pattern that doesn't clash with the Pizzaman box."
- "You get yourself some crystal vases. I'll get an air-hockey table and we'll call it even."

- "Were you deprived as a girl, or what?"
- "I had no idea that shopping with you would rival dental surgery."
- "Screw the towels. I like drying off by rolling on the carpet."
- "Hey, whatever has the best resale value."

The Gift Registration Quiz

The registering process is not over until about the third year of the marriage, when you've either received all the desired items, returned some desired items for others you wanted more, or simply forgot what the hell you desired in the first place. The following multiple-choice quiz is designed to help you get a handle on your wedding-gift acuity, because the sooner you learn the ropes, the further you are from dangling on the end of one.

Define the following items:

Decanter:

      a. Da guy who sings da prayers at a Jewish service

      b. The way you ride a horse between trot and gallop

      c. An overpriced thing in which to show off your liquor

Fine China:

      a. The Beverly Hills of Beijing

      b. Imposing tariffs against a large Asian nation

      c. Overpriced plates that you will never use

Silver Patterns:
- a. What the Lone Ranger's horse leaves in the sand
- b. The fluctuation of a precious metal on the open market
- c. The decorative style of overpriced utensils that you hide in a closet from potential burglars

Crystal:
- a. First name of barberphobic singer whose hit "Make My Brown Eyes Blue" captured the hearts of forlorn lovers everywhere
- b. Street slang for a certain methamphetamine
- c. Overpriced cups that make cool tones when you flick 'em

Bath Sheet:
- a. Accidental turd-floaters that pop out while you're trying to fart in the tub
- b. What you spread out when your fiancée makes you sleep in the bathroom
- c. An overpriced big towel

Gravy Boat:
- a. The other thing you'll be riding for the rest of your life as you mooch off her family's large fortune
- b. Seminal hippie's ocean transport vehicle
- c. An overpriced container for meat juice

Demitasse Cups:
- a. What went to Double D when husband Bruce Willis paid the plastic surgeon
- b. What French midget baseball players wear to protect their testicles
- c. Overpriced, undersized coffee mugs

Scoring: This system is easy. If you answered (a) or (b) to any of the questions, it is recommended that you return to a local department store and study harder. If you answered (c) to *all* the questions, give yourself a firm slap on the back, you should feel totally empowered. Now run along, we're sure your fiancée has something for you to do.

The Food

Your fiancée seems a little uptight. Actually she's as uptight as Roseanne's G-string. But for a change, your bride-to-be has good reason to be on the tense side. She has begun to realize that this wedding is no longer about the two of you. It's about how she will be judged by a jury of her friends, family, in-laws, and a host of assorted others. And as everyone knows, what all the guests come away from the wedding talking about, right after the drunken relative who blows zinfandel out his nose, is the *food*. There are no two ways about it, this crowd has just sat through a long ceremony and is damn hungry. (They have also fasted for days in preparation for a sumptuous spread.) So, if the food isn't good, the whole shindig falls apart.

What we are saying here is that selecting the guy who makes the food is as important to this wedding as the right rodeo clown is to a bull rider. If he doesn't do his job, you get a faceful of bull. So consider carefully the following when meeting and deciding on the right caterers.

Do Not Hire a Caterer Who

- Hates show tunes
- Wears a wedding ring
- Shows up late for your appointment in a Burger King uniform
- Mentions that he ate up a storm in England last summer
- Offers to measure your inseam
- Takes notes on Denny's napkins

- Informs you that wearing pants constricts his creativity
- Gives credit for everything he knows to Mrs. Paul
- Gets angry calls from the FDA every fifteen minutes
- Giggles every time you mention the word "elegant"
- Heartily suggests an insect motif
- Keeps telling you that the "breakfast burrito" isn't just for breakfast anymore
- Insists that the main courses be served with nipple rings

The "Fabu" Food Quiz

After you hire a caterer, you will be invited to taste some masterful creations. This is called a "tasting" and is in preparation for the final menu. The names you'll be hearing for food will make you shake your head. The prices will make it swivel off your neck and roll down the street. As in most planning situations, remember that information is your only ally, right after cash and a few choice photos used for blackmail purposes.

Respond true *or* false *to the following statements.*

CROSTINI are the pieces of fungus you find between your toes.

Answer: False. *Crostini are cheese and anchovies on Italian bread baked with a garlic-flavored melted butter, which may or may not look and smell the same as said fungus.*

TARAMASALATA is what an old man says to his wife when he can't chew his salad.

Answer: False. *Taramasalata is a Greek-style caviar dip, but no matter how old you are, the price for this one will be hard to swallow.*

BRIOCHE is the stickpin accessory Grandma is so fond of wearing.

Answer: False. *A brioche is a lightly baked pastry that Grandma is fond of when she is slightly baked.*

CONSOMMÉ is what you do to the marriage on the first occasion you get your new bride alone.

Answer: False. *Consommé is a simple soup served first at a formal occasion, where slurping sounds are equally frowned upon.*

FRITTO MISTO is the wife-battering, vegetative brother in *The Godfather.*

Answer: False. *Fritto Misto is batter-fried vegetables.*

FRUIT COMPOTE is a rude, albeit often used, description of one of America's foremost authors.

Answer: False. *Fruit compote is a stewed, albeit often served, American fruit mixture.*

QUICHE is what you'll want the caterer to do to your ass after he tells you his rates.

Answer: False. *Quiche is actually the light egg-based pastry that your caterer probably eats all the time.*

PATÉ is what you want to do like it's 1999.

Answer: False. *Paté is finely ground meat, which, if you eat too much, will make you sit on the toilet until 1999.*

Scoring: Unlike the previous quiz, you were not supposed to know any of these items. If you managed to answer any of these questions correctly, take a moment to beat yourself senseless with lightly braised lamb shank in a pleasant honey-dill soubise and pray to the Almighty that none of your friends find out about this.

The Officiant

The selection of an officiant—the person who conducts the matrimonial ceremony—is one of the most crucial decisions you will ever make in your entire life. Having a stammering crony whose powers were vested in him by a state of incoherence will have rippling effects throughout both sides of the family. (One word can sum up the consequences—disowned.) Never risk using the services of anyone who is not a top-notch professional. Yes, that even excludes the friendly chap you met over malted beverages, even though he's presided over two yacht christenings and the burial of his mom's spaniel. The person who knows how to tie the proverbial knot for you two should not claim to have tied a woman's tubes, tied one on, tie-dyed shirts, or tied for first in a one-legged race.

Though a solid five-minute set of nun-with-a-javelin-through-her-head jokes might be welcomed, stick with our simple rule of thumb. Your clergyman or rabbi or judge should be humorless, long-winded, and able to reduce an excited, potentially inebriated crowd to tears of boredom with poorly misguided tales of your love for each other.

Do Not Suggest a
Clergyman/Rabbi/Judge Who

- Loves to play "guess what I'm wearing under my robe?"
- Has an image of Mayor McCheese on his city certificate
- Asks to measure your inseam
- Carries more than one beeper
- Requests at least one Juicy Fruit break during the ceremony
- Keeps speaking of his glory days in Waco, Texas
- Immediately offers you a family discount on embalming
- Won't stop asking, "Are you sure you ain't a cop?"
- Keeps suggesting the time-honored tradition of animal sacrifice
- Wants to hold a premarital conference at Amateur Night at Hooters
- Asks if you have any single grandmothers
- Refers to God as "that bitchin' dude in the sky"
- Stores fake passports in his Bible
- Wants to have a little spiritual retreat with all male cousins under the age of twelve
- Won't stop reaching for a hip flask of "holy spirits"

Free Therapy

A Word-Association Exercise

To help you save on costly psychiatry bills, we are proud to provide a much needed mental-health service. This exercise, created in association with the National Board of Head-shrinkers and Psychobabblers, will allow you to understand your current state of subconscious tension. Lie back on your couch and jot down the first thing that comes to mind when you hear or think of the following phrases.

1. Wall-to-wall carpeting = _____

2. Monday morning = _____

3. Figure drawings = _____

4. Electric toasters = _____

5. Political prisoners = _____

Now, if you are emotionally sound, your fiancée's name should be written in all five spaces. If it is not, you should try to set aside about a C-note a week for the proper counseling. Your progress is deemed much too slow for our realm of expertise.

The Vows

You are certainly entitled to use the standard old vows or whatever drivel your officiant has to offer. But take a moment to think about the possible rewards of surprising your bride with a unique and creative expression of your love. Ponder the possibilities. She might let you pick out paint for the bathroom or give you a say in when you're having children. She might even fall in love with you for real. Hey, the mere mention that you're preparing a special marriage vow might get you a "cheap grab" on the spot. You never know until you try.

We know that you are swamped and you don't have a spare second. Don't fret your handsome little head. With our From-the-Heart Vows™ Kit, you don't need much time at all to write your bride the most personal wedding vows of all time.

From-the-Heart Vows™

Fill in the following items, then plug into the appropriate numbered spaces in the marriage vow.

1._____ (your name)
2._____ (bride's name)
3._____ (name of an organ in the body)
4._____ (your favorite item of clothing—specific)
5._____ (a protective sports item)
6._____ (a sex toy)
7._____ (a bodily function—verb)
8._____ (her favorite group of animals)
9._____ (a feminine hygiene product)
10._____ (her least favorite dessert item)
11._____ (her least favorite type of music)
12._____ (an unusual emotion)
13._____ (a sexual action—verb)
14._____ (a living ex-president—full name)
15._____ (her least favorite sitcom)
16._____ (an insecure area of her body)
17._____ (an everyday activity—verb)

I, (#1), take (#2) to be my wife, knowing in my (#3) that you will be my constant (#4), my faithful (#5) in life, and my one true (#6). On this special day, I (#7) to you in the presence of God and all those (#8) in attendance that I'll stay by your side as your faithful (#9), in sickness and in (#10), in joy and in (#11). I promise to love you without (#12), to honor and (#13) you, to protect you from (#14), to comfort you in times of (#15), to grow with you in mind and (#16), and to cherish you for as long as we both shall (#17).

The Band

From swing to salsa to soul, music is magical (as is alliteration). And as your bride will constantly tell you, usually on the way to someone else's wedding to *audition* a potential band, the right music really makes a party happen. Of course, that's when the tunes are played by musicians who see a bar mitzvah as a place to hit on Jewish chicks and not as a place to earn rent money banging out Leo Sayer medleys.

You see, unless your bride's maiden name is Rockefeller, the band you can afford is going to be a cross between Sonny Bono and Bozo the Clown, and we're not talking about their good, old stuff either. Wedding bands are the bottom feeders in the entertainment tank. They suck the plankton off those guys that "warm up" the audiences for talk shows.

The most you can hope for is that your band's drummer doesn't belch up his hors d'oeuvres until after your grandparents have lost what little hearing they had left from the blaring wall of speakers. The following list is only a partial collection of attributes your band should definitely not embody. Study them closely and beware.

Do Not Suggest a Band That

- Loves show tunes
- Asks to be paid in hard liquor
- Believes that playing a washboard and gin jar is traditional
- "Hava Na what?"
- Lead singer's name is Meatloaf
- During your preliminary meeting with the band in their tour bus, an old lady shouts out, "Hey, you missed my stop!"
- Reminisces about the wild years when they would bite the heads off the chicken l'orange
- Requests space for an Amnesty International booth by the side of the stage, next to their T-shirt stand
- Asks if you supply your own laser show
- Breaks into the hustle the minute you meet them
- Insists that "joint rolling" comes just after your first dance and just before the throwing of the bouquet
- Calls your fiancée "Daddy-o"
- Wants to hand out backstage passes to a few "select babes"
- Features a tambourine player who sporadically shouts out "I am the Lizard King!"
- Brags about featuring two guys who were in the 1987 lineup of Menudo

Fight Break

Fight Topic: Random Frustration

YOU: Knock, knock.

YOUR FIANCÉE: Who's there?

YOU: *(silence)*

YOUR FIANCÉE: Who's there?

YOU: *(silence)*

YOUR FIANCÉE: Come on. Who's there?

YOU: *(silence)*

YOUR FIANCÉE: This isn't funny.

YOU: I just wanted you to know how I feel.

The Documentation

You are going to be too stressed out actually to remember your wedding. So you might as well get some quality photos of the damn thing. And good photos means not assigning picture-taking duties to an overzealous relative who loves to yell the word "cheese." For this you must go to a professional or, shall we say, a frustrated artist/photojournalist who enjoys the finer things in life and needs you to pay for them.

There are many types of wedding photographers. Unfortunately, each maintains a similar showroom and displays a similar book of extremely similar pictures of extremely similar weddings. One way to choose is to opt for the photographer who has the largest sofa-sized blowups of his work. The fact is that unless any of the following happens when you interview the guy, at the end of this whole experience your wife should have a nice monogrammed photo album to show dinner guests who already don't know when it's time to leave.

Do Not Select a Photographer Who

- Is overheard shouting at an assistant, "There's no way in hell I forgot to load the film this time"
- Suggests a round of preceremony shots in the buff
- Drives up in a *Hard Copy* van
- Believes that the birdie to be smiled at lives in his shorts
- Likes to use "a bunch a lit matches" instead of a flash
- Says he will not hesitate to "rip a loud one" if your grandparents won't smile
- Constantly assures you that the "snuff film" charges were dropped
- Tells you that his ceremony behavior is modeled after Dennis Hopper's character in *Apocalypse Now*
- Wears mirrors on his shoes and insists that the future bride stand on a stack of old phone books
- Brags that he can change a camera lens in complete darkness, like, let's say, under a blanket in the back of a moving Chevy
- Shows you samples of his work in *Guns n' Ammo*
- Keeps the door to his darkroom open so he can see what he's doing
- Has you and your family yell out, "Cock-sucking motherfucking Cheez Wiz," instead of a simple "cheese"
- After every flash he drops into a fetal position and cries, "Incoming!"
- For an extra fifty bucks will do the flowers, cut the cake, park cars, and play saxophone

Fight Break

Fight Topic: The Video

YOUR FIANCÉE: I think we should get my cousin Willy to do the video.

YOU: Are you feeling all right?

YOUR FIANCÉE: Willy's perfect for the job.

YOU: Sure, if you consider time spent in prison as work experience.

YOUR FIANCÉE: Come on, he was only in for a year.

YOU: Wow, maybe if we're lucky, Willy can narrate the whole thing using euphemisms he learned in the big house.

YOUR FIANCÉE: We'd be saving a lot of money.

YOU: Not if you consider all the missing watches and wallets.

YOUR FIANCÉE: Willy's changed. Videography is his life.

YOU: Well, I guess his permanently trembling limbs could make our video look like a good episode of *NYPD Blue*.

YOUR FIANCÉE: Enough with the prison jokes already.

YOU: Hey, if the felony fits. . . .

YOUR FIANCÉE: We need a videographer, smarty, and we can't afford the going rates.

YOU: Why don't we ask my uncle Paul with tuberculosis. We can get a great batch of reaction shots around the tables as he coughs huge lung cookies into the centerpieces. Or better yet, what about your friend Lucille, the one with cataracts. Or how about—

YOUR FIANCÉE: Fine. We just won't have a video for our children to watch.

YOU: Great, so does Willy still need to be invited then?

The Best Man

Selecting a best man may be the closest you'll ever come to admitting your love for a male friend. (Well, except for that one night you spent in a Mexican prison.) Whoever you choose will have to take the job very seriously. You must find someone you can trust, someone you can turn to in a time of need, someone who won't try to seduce your wife in a coat closet.

To assist you in this decision, one of the few that will be solely up to you, we have provided a simple chart of the pros and cons for each of the typical best-man contenders.

Prospect	Pros	Cons
Brother	He won't dare reveal bachelor party secrets because you know too many of his	It looks like you have no friends
College best friend	Can talk you down from any bad trip	Your high school best friend will be hurt
High school best bud	His wacky toast topics can only include gym class and SAT tests	Your college best friend will be hurt
Great-looking pal	All the bridesmaids will love him	Your bride might love him
Cross-dressing cousin	You'll be complimented for forward thinking	He might clash with the bride
Your bookie	He'll be close at hand for all the games you're missing that night	He may pawn wedding bands as payment for future losses
Your invisible friend Billy	It will mean a lot to him	He's kinda shy and might screw up his toast

Groomsmen Gifts

Imagine your best man and your other groomsmen as your last line of defense. Like a football team huddling their quarterback, they will even be there for you during the stressful pregame when anything can, and will, go wrong. Whether it's a last-minute pep talk or a ride to the church or even a firm spank on the tush, they will give you what you need. In return, you must give them a token of your appreciation comparable to the selfless goodwill you will receive from them.

When choosing an appropriate gift for your groomsmen, it is best to stick with the traditional symbols of masculine bonhomie. Look for something that says, "You, my friend, have done me well. I salute you." Something like a handsome leather wallet or fine silver flask. As a good rule of thumb, it is best to avoid gifts that are either excessively flamboyant, ridiculously cheap, or still breathing. While by no means complete, the list below consists of gifts that are considered verboten for all but the most intrepid groomsman — and even then they should be used only with extreme caution.

What Not to Give as Groomsmen Gifts

- High colonics
- Pictures of your fiancée naked
- A slap on the back and a fortune cookie
- A promise that you'll give them something at your next wedding
- Your therapy bills
- A subway token of your appreciation
- Rooms next to yours at the honeymoon location
- The finger
- Keys to your new home
- Permission to ask your father-in-law for cash
- A certificate to select anything off your registry as their own
- A day with your wife's credit card
- A night with your wife's sister
- First dibs on the centerpieces
- First dibs on the flower girl when she comes of age

The Inquirers

This wedding is starting to wear down your polite exterior. But for relatives, friends, family, gossips, and especially doormen, deli counter guys, and other lonely food-service professionals, once word gets out that you are planning a wedding, you will be forced into more small talk than humanly imaginable. As tempting as it may be to go postal on these tiring busybodies, remember most of them are involuntarily single, old, or both. Humor them with a pleasant retort and your fiancée will respect your restraint. Open up with any of the following barbs, and this time next year you may just find yourself being asked, "How did those breakup plans go?"

How Not to Respond When Asked, "How Are the Wedding Plans Going?"

- "I'm thinking of having myself put to sleep."
- "Plans? Well, I plan on getting one big-ass present from you, that's what I'm planning."
- "I love wedding planning. It's really fun . . . I love wedding planning. It's really fun . . . I love wedding planning. . . ."
- "For the price of four hubcaps and a quart of oil, it's going to be one helluva bash."
- "I don't really care, my bitch is handling the whole thing."
- "The next person who asks gets a fist in the gut. Got that, Grandma?"

- "Let's put it this way. I won't be able to sit comfortably for weeks."
- "Does the word 'elope' mean anything to you?"
- "It's going fine, if you like ulcers and lots of them."
- "What do you care? You're not invited."
- "Hey, there's nothing more fulfilling than flowers and chicken."
- "The plan? The plan is for her parents to take over the entire production, then hold the cost over my head for all eternity."

Fight Topic: The Guest List

YOUR FIANCÉE: We have way too many people on the guest list.

YOU: So, what do a few more hurt?

YOUR FIANCÉE: Do you have any idea how much this little wedding is costing?

YOU: Yes, because you keep telling me.

YOUR FIANCÉE: It's a pretty big sum, and therefore you have to cut down on the frivolous invites.

YOU: Manny and Joe, my mechanics, are not frivolous.

YOUR FIANCÉE: They were the mechanics for your *last* car.

YOU: They still have feelings.

YOUR FIANCÉE: Fine. Invite Manny and Joe, but you'll have to cut down somewhere else.

YOU: Well if you're going to nitpick, then I think you should count your aunt Delores as two people, she's so damn fat.

YOUR FIANCÉE: Oh, that's constructive.

YOU: How do you think I feel? It's my wedding and the only people who are guaranteed to be invited are family members that we never see, and secretly despise, and my parents' friends who have done the wonderful favor of seeing me grow up and thus are owed the pleasure of getting a free gourmet meal and watching me dance with a woman they have never met. Then, and only then, do I get to select a few friends. Friends who are only legitimate choices if they see me more than twice in the months that end in "r," if they live in town, or call me, on their phone bills, once a week if they live away. And even then, if they happen to be going out with somebody, their stock plummets inordinately.

YOUR FIANCÉE: Family friends give great gifts.

YOU: Okay.

The Invitation

Wouldn't it be really cool if you had silhouetted women on your wedding invitation like on those truck mudflaps and your response cards were shaped like beer bottles? Yeah, we know. It will never happen while your fiancée is still drawing in air. So as a token of our sympathy, we submit for your enjoyment the following invitation. It might be as close to perfection as you ever get.

Mr. and Mrs. Joe Smith

cordially invite you,

and only you,

and not that live-in lover or your brother's cousin

or some business associate you need to impress,

to the betrothal of their daughter

Amy "I'm now taken by a stud"

to

Joe "The Tubeman"

son of

The Royal Duke and Duchess Camposola

on

the only Saturday the church had free

(and just before she started showing)

End of the Millennium

6:00 PM until the pigs 'n blankets run out or Mass begins

Mastercard/VISA Accepted   Dress: Optional

No RSVP'S — "Don't call us, we'll call you"

B.Y.O.B.

The Mailing

You are at your wit's end. You've tried to be a good groom. You've nodded your head at all the right moments. You've been extremely pleasant with your future in-laws even when they keep getting your name wrong. But you don't know how much longer you can take it. Then the invitations come back from the printer and you find yourself sitting at her parents' house looking at a vast paper wasteland. Spread out before you are invites, RSVP cards, envelopes, and stamps. Her dad puts on his favorite Lawrence Welk album—"The early sessions, before he sold out"—and the whole gang sits down to stuff and seal envelopes.

"C'mon," says her perky mom, "it'll be fun. We will create an assembly line and we'll be done in no time. Then afterward, if you kids are good, Dad will take you out for some Baskin Robbins." You want to rip off your head. You want to scream that Baskin Robbins isn't even cool because it was the last chain to figure out people wanted fat-free yogurt. You know you must stay calm, but if you actually have to sit down with these people and seal envelopes, somebody is going to be sealing a body bag before the night is over.

Never fear. With this easy-to-use, self-assembling wheel of excuses, you won't have to do a thing. Just cut it out, spin it on your finger, and say, "I'd love to help, but. . . ."

The Wheel of Excuses

Fight Topic: The Flower Girl and the Ring Bearer

YOUR FIANCÉE: I want my cousin Amy to be our flower girl.

YOU: Yeah, and I want a new television.

YOUR FIANCÉE: It'll be great. We can have your cousin Petey be the ring bearer.

YOU: I wouldn't let that little squirt rip paper towels in the men's room.

YOUR FIANCÉE: Come on. It'll be so sweet to have them both there.

YOU: To have them hung from trees and beaten like piñatas, maybe.

YOUR FIANCÉE: Amy can throw floral petals and—

YOU: —and your grandma can slip and rupture a tendon on the way out.

YOUR FIANCÉE: You're so unromantic.

YOU: If having two hyperactive, spoiled spawns of Satan careening down the runway throwing mangled floral items, then I guess so.

YOUR FIANCÉE: You know, I've always dreamed of having a flower girl.

YOU: Me too, but then I always get arrested in the middle of it and wake up.

YOUR FIANCÉE: I can call this whole thing off right now if it's making you so uncomfortable.

YOU: Having children in the wedding ceremony is making me uncomfortable.

YOUR FIANCÉE: Oh, so what's wrong with children?

YOU: Nothing if they stay away from you.

YOUR FIANCÉE: So when were you going to tell me you hated kids?

YOU: Before the first trimester, I guess.

The Tuxedo

You would think you're old enough to dress yourself, that this would be one area you could handle. You go in and rent a tux. You put it on. The crowd cheers, and it's off to the honeymoon. As the Beach Boys crooned so sadly, "Wouldn't it be nice." The tuxedo procurement portion of your wedding is treacherous. The tuxedo peddler will tell you one thing, your fashion sense another, and, as always, all that really matters is what your bride tells you.

Of course, you always dreamed that you'd get married in Vegas, wearing your Steelers sweatshirt and your favorite Donald Duck boxers. And after you suggested the purple lamé tuxes for your groomsmen, she thought she was seeing a humorous side to you that she had never noticed. When she realized you were serious, she commenced worrying. When you mentioned the beer-bottles-from-around-the-world suspenders, she put in a call to Mom.

No need to fret. Here is a touch of advice to assist you in righting the potential wrongs of tuxedo shopping. And believe us, all penguins are not alike (although they all do taste like chicken). The moneyed relatives take dress into consideration when endorsing those gift checks, so pay close attention.

Do Not Select a Tuxedo Shop That

- Is located in the back of an AM/PM store
- Displays its sample formal wear on cadavers
- Has a sign in the window that reads, "Free mammogram with every rental"
- Makes salespeople dress as their favorite character from *The Rocky Horror Picture Show*
- Offers you a choice of soup or salad the minute you enter
- Employs a salesman who winks and asks, "Is that a roll of quarters in your rented pants or are you just happy to see me?"
- Measures your neck size with a damp Popsicle stick
- Sells solid-gold cuff links in the shape of an annulment certificate
- Does its best business on Halloween
- Offers to remove unsightly tummy bulges with an industrial steam cleaner in the back room
- Specializes in "edible trousers"
- Was recommended to you by your bookie
- Also rents celebrity look-alike groomsmen for a nominal fee
- Believes no outfit is complete without a tiara of fresh heather
- Guarantees a perfect fit or it will dress your next wedding for free

The Ideal Look

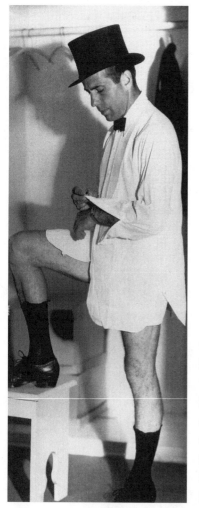

A Formal-Wear Doll

Select the items that go on the ideal groom.

1. Jacket
2. Party hat
3. Flippers
4. Cummerbund
5. Tutu
6. Heated socks
7. Butt-plug
8. Sunglasses
9. Tux shirt
10. Platform shoes
11. Parachute
12. Bow tie
13. Back brace

Correct choices: Flippers for wading through the quagmire of phony socializing; heated socks for warming cold feet; butt-plug for protection during last-minute bill calculations; sunglasses for stemming the glare of major scrutiny; parachute for bailing out if party goes into a tailspin; back brace for lugging around family baggage in public.

Fight Break

Fight Topic: The Seating

YOU: Let 'em all sit where they want. I hate assignments.

YOUR FIANCÉE: You are so classless.

YOU: *(belching loudly)*: No I ain't.

YOUR FIANCÉE: Come on, I've almost got everyone seated according to age or relationship to the family. We just have to find a place for your friends.

YOU: Don't worry. They'll be sucking back so much free booze they'll never know if the person they're next to is dead or your aunt Lucille.

YOUR FIANCÉE: Oh, that's a help.

YOU: You're right. Aunt Lucille and a dead person are too similar. What about a flaming auto wreck and—

YOUR FIANCÉE: Enough. Just give me the list of your friends.

YOU: I *actually* got to invite people I know?

YOUR FIANCÉE: Give me their names now or I'll disinvite them.

YOU: Look. There are like twenty-five of them. Tables seat eight, so we can draw names from a hat for the three tables. And toss the extra to one of the other tables.

YOUR FIANCÉE: Really? What happens if the extra one is Danny or Bob? Everyone hates those guys.

YOU: Not true. But I'll make Dickie the extra.

YOUR FIANCÉE: He always smells funny.

YOU: Okay. Greg.

YOUR FIANCÉE: My friends think he has a personality disorder.

YOU: What about Stan? He's a little artsy. We can stick him with your cousins, the pottery makers.

YOUR FIANCÉE: Then that throws off that whole table. It's all people in housewares, you know.

YOU: How about me and Aunt Lucille drink ourselves sick and one of my friends eats dinner with you at the head table?

The Table Assignments

Since both families will want a say in where their guests are seated at the reception, formalizing the table assignments can be the greatest challenge your newly "joined" clans will face. It will rank right up there with stuffing Grandma into her corset and keeping Dad from hitting the sauce too early. To attack the problem logically, your fiancée might use index cards or a bulletin board or have the residents of a nearby retirement home come over to map out the seating in real space. Any which way, the mathematics will never work to everyone's liking since as of yet there is no way to fit six couples at an eight-seater table, even if they all suffer from rickets. No matter how you swap and switch and squeeze, a few "odds 'n ends" guests will be left without a place to sit.

To deal with these dilemmas effectively, and without creating irreparable damage to the congealing familial cohesion, you must rethink the way you're handling the situation. Everyone present at your strategy session should take turns trying to match up a "troublesome" guest from Column A to a uniquely grouped table from Column B where the person is best suited. This is guaranteed to open up new passageways in your minds and allow you to find places to stick those seatless, loser invitees.

Column A

Odds 'n Ends

1. Cousin who can't hold down a steady job

2. Ethnically "different" couple

3. The priest

4. Aunt with Tourette's syndrome

5. Prematurely bald college pal

6. Newly widowed lady

7. Harriet the hermaphrodite

8. Uncle who lost his nose in the war

9. The hairdresser

10. Cousin who loves to show off her boob job

Column B

Table Groupings

a. Incontinent old people

b. People who have recently suffered catastrophic loss

c. Newlywed table

d. People who are gay but don't know it yet

e. Weight-challenged people

f. Cancer survivors

g. Elderly relatives with glaucoma

h. Unhappily married couples

i. Rich old people with no heirs

j. Couples who go both ways

Answer Key:

1-i, 2-g, 3-b, 4-e, 5-f, 6-c, 7-j, 8-a, 9-d, 10-h

Chapter Three

The Festivities

'Til Death Do Us Party

The Bachelor Party

There comes a moment in every man's life when he must venture out into the uncharted regions of the netherworld and discover the answers to life's three unsolved questions: Why am I here? Where am I going? What's the best way to remove a bra with your teeth? The proper forum for this existential soul-searching is, of course, the bachelor party.

Your bachelor party is the last splash in a, hopefully, long and illustrious career of champagne-filled, panty-strewn, prophylactic-laced bachelor living. It is a time to throw caution and vomit to the wind and learn interesting new ways to serve a Ping-Pong ball. Sadly, your fiancée will probably be less than excited about this prospect. It will be up to you to reassure her that this gathering is as natural as a circle of onlookers is after a successful high-rise suicide. This will not be easy, but with all you've had to endure in the name of wedding planning, you owe it to yourself to slip this one by her.

There are many different routes to choose when convincing your fiancée of the need for this bacchanalian feast. Here are several scripts to recite, for if one doesn't work, move right into the next one, and the next one and. . . .

The Declaration of Your Independence

"When in the course of human events it becomes necessary for a man to give up that which nature tells him is his forever . . . I'm speaking of life, liberty, and the pursuit of short-skirted coeds. It becomes necessary to give up this freedom, for a woman whose charms know no boundaries, whose smile is brighter than all the lights at Times Square, whose wit challenges the world's greatest comics. We, the couple, must together realize that this man must have what to some is called a party. To some, this 'party' is fun and games, an excuse to dally in the depths of man's soul. Ahhh, but to this particular man, this so-called party is much less. Not a party, but a funeral for his old and terrible ways and a birthday for his new clean and changed life."

The Bill Shakespeare

"To me the only question that really lies before us is the age-old question . . . to tip or not to tip. Whether 'tis nobler to kneel 'neath a strumpet and giveth her a dollar bill, or sit handcuffed to a chair whilst a woman wearing a police uniform thrusts her feminine wiles in thine face. Get thee to a nunnery, I would tell any such tramp and that which would occur would be for naught."

The Mr. Nice Guy

"Look, I owe this to my friends. They need this party. If it were up to me, I wouldn't even think of having a bachelor party. But that wouldn't be right. All my friends are so jealous, I have got the most beautiful perfect woman in the world and what do they have? Nothing. They need this ritual. And I say ritual in the truest religious sense of the word. All a bachelor party is, is a way for my friends to mourn my loss from their world. Anything crazy that they have planned, they can be a part of. Me, I want to have a drink and a cigar and come right home to you. Hey, if it were up to me, you could even come to the party. Just a little steak, a bit of single-malt scotch. My mind is with you the whole time."

The Reverse Psychologist

"Bachelor party, oh no, not me. I would much rather be made fun of by all my friends then actually have one of those Neanderthal, pointless games going on for me. I would rather be called a spineless pussy-whipped shell of a man than have to sit there while some silicon-enhanced tramp flaunts herself so my friends can have one last good time in front of me. No thank you, ma'am. I don't care if our whole marriage is put in jeopardy because my lifelong buddies (who would take a bullet for me) feel that my new wife is a controlling bitch. No sireee. For one last laugh with the guys? I don't think so."

The Subliminal Schtick
(Words in parentheses are said under your breath)

"So listen, honey, it's not gonna be much of a party (honeymoon is coming up). It'll be me and a couple of my friends (they have to give us presents) having a nice dinner (remember how much that ring cost me). I know what you have heard about these things (house in the country) but it's not really like that (your older sister's still single). It's a funny old tradition (we're getting a joint checking account), but a strong tradition nonetheless (once we've had kids, you'll never work again). So I'm glad you understand (joint savings!!!). You won't regret it."

The Last Hope

"Please, please. All the other guys got to have bachelor parties. Please, I will look dumb in front of all my friends. Pretty please. I'll be your best friend. C'mon, you can go to Chippendales. I don't care. Spread hot oil on some Fabio looking guy named Thor. Please. I have been looking forward to this all my life. C'mon, you picked all the china and stuff."

The Do-It-Yourself Bachelor Party™

Okay, we realize that in today's "modern" society, there are women who find the idea of a bachelor party so archaic, so offensive, and so degrading that they will effectively stop their guy from participating in one. In other words, your begging didn't work. We also know that there are men who will actually abide by their fiancée's mandate and forgo the festivities promised to them by birth and thus refuse to lie and have a bachelor party anyway. Well, for these "modern" men we are proud to offer this realistic, easy-to-follow, Do-It-Yourself Bachelor Party™. No assembly required. Items needed: 1 can whipped cream, 1 bottle tequila, 1 cigar.

1. Laminate the following page.
2. Find an old sitcom on TV. Everytime anyone on the show says the word "the," you drink a shot of tequila. Add your own rules like drinking the entire bottle every time someone other than Mr. Jefferson says "Weesy."
3. Laugh heartily. Pretend you're playing drinking games with people other than just yourself.
4. Smoke the cigar.
5. Say out loud, "Good thing there are no women here. Women hate the smell of these cigars, huh boys?"
6. Curse.
7. Take a look at the picture on this page.
8. Say aloud, "You guys are too much. Who bought the babe?"

9. Squirt some whipped cream on the appropriate parts of the girl's picture.
10. Take out a couple of ten dollar bills and burn them.
11. Now you can lick the whipped cream off, but don't let your tongue linger too long. That costs extra.
12. Shout some more curses.
13. Vomit.
14. Pass out.
15. Wake up and tell your fiancée that nothing happened.

The Aftermath

As with any form of jungle warfare on foreign soil, *what happens in the bush, stays in the bush.* Even in the face of guilt, shame, and stubborn crab infestation, you must resist the temptation to tell your fiancée anything about the true nature of the evening's events.

Because this strict code of silence is an essential commodity in the preservation of your future happiness and sanity, destroy any and all compromising souvenirs—photos, videos, small farm animals—and never, we repeat, never allow the following statements to pass from your lips.

What Not to Say to Your Fiancée after the Bachelor Party

- "I just dropped a dollar bill. Do you think you can pick that up without using your hands?"
- "Is it possible to push the wedding ceremony back a day? I've got this nagging headache."
- "You know, leg harnesses aren't as uncomfortable as they look."
- "Ever heard of Kegels?"

- "Did you know we're out of whipped cream?"
- "We never stay home and rent movies anymore."
- "I think I should be able to straighten my back in about a week."
- "Have you seen the car?"
- "Have change for twenty? I'm fresh out of singles."
- "Can you explain that whole fidelity trip again?"
- "Damn, my tongue hurts."
- "Want to see my new tattoo?"
- "I invested all our savings in silicon this morning."
- "Have you seen my liver?"
- "Can you pick the lock on these handcuffs?"
- "I'd like you to meet my new best man . . . Mr. Jack Daniel's."
- "K-Y jelly washes out, doesn't it?"
- "We might have a new addition to the family in about nine months."
- "Your father has himself some damn sexy legs."
- "I'm thinking about having one of these shindigs every year."

The Rehearsal

The big day is twenty-four hours away and you'd like nothing more than to curl up on your BarcaLounger with a cold draft and an HBO special. Unfortunately, no event as monumental as a wedding comes off without a dry run. Whether you think it's needed or not, you'll get a dress rehearsal, just without the dress, if you will. And you will; you have no choice.

Presiding over these festivities will be the clergyman, or location's coordinator, or head of the household, or, in some extreme cases, Captain Stubing. Try to relax. This exercise should require little exertion on your part. Simply watch as the wedding party is told how to enter, where to stand, and what to eat for breakfast that doesn't cause flatus. Enjoy the sight of groomsmen and bridesmaids, flirting and preening and gazing in wonderment at your father's choice of leisure-suit color.

If you keep your eyes open and your mouth closed, you will be able to appreciate the incredible energy that surrounds and embraces a loving couple on the threshold of matrimony. Take it all in while you can. It is yours for only a short time more.

What Not to Say to the
Coordinator at the Rehearsal

- "You know, I banged her on our second date."
- "There's no way my friends are escorting those beasts down the aisle."
- "You know how there's 'something old, something new, something borrowed.' . . . Can my balls count for the 'something blue'?"
- "Damn me to hell, that shipment of pure grain alcohol should've been here already."
- "Tuxedo? Holy shit, nobody told me about a wearing a tuxedo."
- "Screw the 'Wedding March,' let's use the rap classic 'Rump Shaker.'"
- "Can we line the altar with newspaper, like a bird cage? I've been known to lose my bladder when I'm nervous."
- "Don't you think this wedding canopy would look great shoved up my mother-in-law's ass?"
- "Where do my other wives stand?"
- "Can I smoke during the service?"
- "Mention God again and I slice your throat out, fat boy."
- "When you say, '. . . Speak now or forever hold your piece,' about what piece are you speaking? Because I'm pretty sure that can cause blindness."

Rehearsal Tips

The rehearsal is also a good time to inform the groomsmen who are to be ushers at the ceremony exactly how you want them to perform their critical duties. Should they seat guests by affiliation to the families? By time of arrival? By smell? It's a personal decision but one that needs to be made before the big day. Then, things will be flying past you so fast you'll think you're a supermodel at a Book-of-the-Month-Club reading.

No matter how busy you are perspiring, take the necessary moments to bring your noble gentlemen up to speed. The chart that follows is intended only as a guide; it is not meant to serve as formal legislation. As with all endeavors that involve walking, extreme caution is recommended.

Ushers Should	Ushers Should Not
Ask, "Are you with the bride's side or the groom's?"	Exclaim, "Judging by that gap in your teeth, I'd say you're with the bride's side."
Clear a path.	Clear a path and yell, "Wide load comin' through!"
Kindly say, "Hello, I'll be escorting you to your seat today."	Kindly say, "Hello, I'll be escorting you to your seat today. Don't touch me."
Offer emotional guests Kleenex.	Offer the emotionless words, "If you cry at all during the ceremony, you'll be forcibly removed."
Whisper, "Please follow me to the front of the chapel."	Whisper, "Please follow me to the 'had to be invited' section."
Mention, "Perhaps you would like to sign the guest book before I seat you."	Mention, "Perhaps you would like to take a shower with me before I seat you."
Tell late arrivers, "Although it's crowded, there's always a place for you."	Tell late arrivers, "All the good seats are taken. But well, um, maybe if your friend Andrew Jackson showed up in my palm."
Remark, "Take your time, ma'am, the ceremony won't start until you're comfortable."	Remark, "Pick up the pace, Grandma. I don't have time for this shit."

The Out-of-Town Guests

Generally, after the rehearsal, a festive meal is given by the groom's parents for the wedding party, the immediate families, and all out-of-town guests. "Wait a minute," you say, "out-of-town guests?" Think back. Remember when you sent out all of those invitations to obscure relatives in far-away places? Well, people will journey across the globe for a slab of meat and a goblet of cheap wine. That's right, you are going to see relatives you would rather not know you had and old friends of your parents you thought were long since deceased. Ready or not, you are going to have to be pleasant to each and every one of them. You are too close to the end of the wedding maze to take an ill-advised turn and miss the reward. If you don't let any of following greetings squeak out, the big man in the lab coat won't give you a high-voltage shock and then dissect you to see what went wrong.

How Not to Greet Out-of-Town Guests
- "Can I see some identification?"
- "Do me a favor, stay away from my friends."
- "I've got two words for you . . . Alcoholics Anonymous."
- "Wow, and here Mom said you had one foot in the grave."

- "I thought you were going to get the hairs removed from that growth the last time you were in town."
- "I hope the plane fare wasn't deducted from the amount you spent on our gift."
- "When we said, 'and guest,' we didn't mean a toupee."
- "Oh, how terrible, you must've lost your luggage."
- "We took the liberty of ordering you a low-fat meal."
- "Don't even think about coming by the house later."
- "So, uh, when's your flight home?"
- "Nice limp."
- "I'm sorry. You looked pregnant."
- "Why didn't you call? I could've lent you a decent tie."
- "This envelope better have more than a card in it."

The Wedding-Day Countdown

A Twenty-Four-Hour Schedule of Events

4:32 AM — Wake from lack of oxygen, remind heart to stop skipping beats.

4:34 AM — Count old girlfriends and try to fall back asleep.

4:38 AM — Masturbate gloomily, roll over, pass out.

6:11 AM — Dream of falling from window while being chased by invisible warlocks, after fleeing a high school final exam because you were unprepared and naked.

7:32 AM — Reawaken from sound of sweat beads hitting pillow.

7:34 AM — Practice wedding toast.

At some point in the reception, you will be inclined to make a small toast, thanking your family for their love, support, blah-bity-blah-blah. You will also find it necessary to offer a few kind words for the people who have made the event possible. No, it's not the Academy of Motion Picture Arts and Sciences; we're talking about your newest source of tax-free revenue—the in-laws. Keep in mind that the persona you present in the formative stages of your road to married life will affect the way you are viewed for decades to follow. For example, a single tear when you toast your new family could mean the difference between a late-model convertible BMW and an '82 Civic with worn brake pads when the wedding present negotiations roll around. As always, the choice is yours.

This toast is time for you to wax eloquent about the wonderful humanitarians who soon will, hopefully, be calling you "son" and not "that worthless mound of flesh." But take care—the toast is nothing if not a sucker's trap. Amid all the roasting and boasting from friends and family, it's easy to get carried away and delude oneself into thinking that tomorrow's "Mom" and "Pop" can actually take today's joking. As far as they're concerned, you are marrying a virgin who still wears jammies to bed. Wedding time is not a suitable occasion to inform them they are crotchless. Just keep your tongue tied and resist the urge to open your toast with any of the following lines.

How Not to Open the Wedding-Night Toast

- "Just think . . . this time last year I was sleeping with anything that moved."
- "Marriage is a sacred tradition in our two families. Then again, so is chemical dependency."
- "You know, last night when I looked at your sleeping daughter, her silky hair draped across her shoulders, her sweet lips glistening in the moonlight, her arms still strapped to the bedposts. . . ."
- "As Don Corleone once said. . . ."
- "I'm so happy that you have set a standard of matrimonial stability that is a shining example for us all. So with that in mind, I'd like to bring out the strippers."
- "On behalf of my entire family, I'd like to welcome your family's financial portfolio."
- "Ooh, me so horny."
- "Although you haven't met my other wives. . . ."
- "Help! Mommy! Help."
- "I'd just like to take a few moments to say a warm, heartfelt good-bye to my sanity."
- "Looking over at my future mother-in-law, I'm reminded that love is indeed blind."
- "There once was a girl from Nantucket. . . ."
- "Thank you so much for raising a woman who understands a man's need to wear panties and high heels."

7:36 AM—Crumble scratch paper and tell yourself that toast will flow better if unrehearsed.

7:37 AM—Get out of bed.

8:12 AM—Fix breakfast (ignore violently cramping stomach muscles).

9:28 AM—Call friends and act composed.

9:29 AM—Run to toilet.

10:32 AM—Take out tuxedo from plastic covering.

10:33 AM—Call family member and make sure someone knows how to dress you.

10:34 AM—Have heart-to-heart chat with mother or mother figure.

For your mother, this wedding is just as much about loss as it is about celebration. You both have that in common. But hers might actually be deeper. You are the product of her love, the apple of her eye, the high-fructose corn syrup in her Honey-Nut Cheerios. And today, she is losing you to another woman. Sure, it sounds rather weird, verging on Oedipal, verging on "I'll never get an erection again," but try to show this woman some compassion. For the moment, set aside petty conflicts or bruised egos or the fact that she flew your pee-stained sheets like a kite on that Fourth of July party where that girl you had a crush on laughed so hard she had to be hospitalized. Your mother is your mother. Let her know that you love her and always will, even if it's a bold-faced, knee-slapping lie. Stave off the hysterical sobbing for later, and do not let dear ol' Mom hear any of the following comments.

What Not to Say to Your Mother on Wedding Day

- "Who invited you?"
- "Did I mention the bride is . . . a man?"
- "Go have a beer and shut up."
- "This is the happiest day of my life. Can I borrow fifty grand?"
- "Just because you raised me doesn't mean you deserve a good table."
- "Why can't you be more like my new mother?"
- "You won't be needing your house much longer, will you?"
- "I hope you're looking forward to meeting the Reverend Moon."
- "Thanks for raising me with so much love and respect. Now how 'bout a new car?"
- "Now listen. I want you and Dad to tumble into the cake so we can win some cash on one of those home-video shows."
- "If two guys with no necks show up looking for me, tell them I left the country."
- "First thing tomorrow I'm going to the methadone clinic."
- "Dance with me and I'll scream."

11:07 AM—Read book, sit in sun, watch TV.
11:43 AM—Enjoy taste of gurgling intestinal acids.
12:50 PM—Lie down for a nap.
12:51 PM—Remember old girlfriends and masturbate gloomily.

2:00 PM—Awake screaming.
2:32 PM—Shower.
2:34 PM—Think of old girlfriends and masturbate
gloomily.
3:11 PM—Get dressed with
plenty of assistance.
3:30 PM—Drive to wed-
ding site.
3:31 PM—Remember that
fiancée told you to be there
at 3:00.
4:00 PM—Line up for photos.
4:15 PM—Take photos.

Your rental shoes are so tight your toes feel like they're coming out of your ankles. Your cummerbund has such a vice grip on your midsection you feel like you need to go to the restroom every thirty seconds. Your shirt has too much starch in the collar, and you're pretty sure that one of your cuff links has severed an artery in your wrist . . . SMILE! Yes, smile wide and with feeling, it's time for an endless run of posed photographs. Let's do one with you and your dad. Now, one with you and *her* dad. Hey, let's try one with your dad and her dad and their dads, all drinking mugs of Dad's Root Beer.

The torture of this bulb-flashing experience rivals anything witnessed since that love scene with Whoopi Goldberg in *Ghost*. We just have two words of advice for you: Say cheese! You do not want to make a fool of yourself just yet and you don't want to make a fool of the photographer until after he's given you the proofs. So, hold tight to your tripod and remember the following:

- Do not make both families form a human pyramid
- Do not cancel the ceremony if you don't get as much makeup as your bride
- Do not request a few boudoir shots with the bridesmaids
- Do not keep asking if your bride's gut is blocking you from the frame
- Do not heckle all grandparents on unsightly ear-hair growth
- Do not remind everyone that you mastered close-up photography at the county lockup
- Do not demand that pictures contain at least one person getting slipped a little tongue
- Do not mention that an old girlfriend will be popping from the wedding cake
- Do not pass out business cards from a major plastic surgeon to the bride's family
- Do not instruct the wedding party that they must also pose for your nude figure drawing class
- Do not remove the photographer's spleen with your hands and use it as a corsage
- Do not draw a mustache on your mother-in-law *before* the photo is processed
- Do not cool the burned flash lights with your underpants
- Do not ask for your bride's body double

4:30 PM — Pray desperately that photos will end.
6:00 PM — Photos end.

6:12 PM—Give CPR to at least one elderly relative in wedding party.

6:30 PM—Ceremony begins.

6:35 PM—The processional.

"Here comes the bride, all dressed in white." Or so goes the classic by a long-dead composer who became a favorite of the Third Reich. Anyway, there will come a fateful moment when your beaming bride will appear, veiled in a radiant glow and a doily over her face. The subsequent graceful glide down the aisle, in front of a room full of loved ones, will be the realization of a dream for the soon-to-be Missus You. It will be the precise rip in time that she has been waiting for ever since the romantic synapses in her brain began to fire or she began to crawl, whichever came first.

If you are a normal male of the species, the ritual "giving away" of the bride by a father or father figure at the end of the processional might stimulate the jokester in you. Hold back, if you can. Try to digest the magnitude of that moment for your bride. Slapping your future father-in-law on the ass and saying, "Thanks for the hand-off, man. I'll spike her when I get to the end zone," will generally get you the business end of a cummerbund. Think how long you'll be standing in one place in front of so many people. Should the urge move you, remember the following:

- Do not holler, "Come on down. You're the next contestant *on* Mr. Right."
- Do not nudge the clergyman and whisper, "I'm not wearing any underpants."
- Do not turn your back and urinate quietly

- Do not yell, "Hey, what the hell are *you* doing here?"
- Do not pull up your shirt and bang out "Here Comes the Bride" on your belly
- Do not contact your bookie on a cell phone
- Do not wonder aloud, "Honey, are you bloating this week or what?"
- Do not call out your bride's every move like a horse-racing announcer
- Do not grab your crotch and yell, "Fat-bottom girl you make my rockin' world go 'round."
- Do not hail a cab
- Do not hum "The Battle Hymn of the Republic"
- Do not auction your bride off to the highest bidder
- Do not comment to the wedding party, "Damn, I've got me some bad gas."
- Do not make all the guests do the wave
- Do not strum fingers across your thigh and blurt, "Can you pick up the pace, toots? I'm starving."

6:45 PM—Take final vows: "I do, I do, for chrissakes. Now will everybody get off my back?" (*Note:* Time is for nondenominational ceremony. Add thirty minutes for every god in your religion.)

7:00 PM—Cocktails.

7:02 PM—Get pulled away for more photos.

7:04 PM—Enjoy guests hollering out their congratulations.

7:09 PM—An aunt slips by photographer gauntlet and pinches your cheeks before getting wrestled to the ground by groomsmen.

7:45 PM—Toasts.

8:21 PM—*Your* toast.

The moment of truth has finally arrived. Sure you thought you could hide behind the bartender and the party would simply proceed without your appearance at the microphone. Don't panic, it's your night. So what, you never really found any more time to practice. Come out from your corner. Nobody is going to judge you if you're less than eloquent. Everybody is there to see you. They don't care what you say.

If you buy that, send us your credit card and we promise not to use it. The sentiments you choose to express on this occasion are as permanent as that headless chicken tattoo you got tricked into getting at your bachelor party. If you verbalize anything but pure, earth-shattering love, your house will enjoy but one holiday a year—Doomsday. Take a second, smile at the gawking onlookers, look into your heart, and quickly eliminate any of the following lines from your oration.

What Not to Include in Your Wedding-Night Toast

- "Could someone throw me a wet-nap, I think I just pissed all over myself."
- "Finally, after so many attempts, I've met a girl who actually said yes."
- "I'd like to take this time to thank the warden for not opening her letters."
- "And even though she slept with my best friend. . . ."
- "In all my swinging single years, I've never been given such a great pipe cleaning."
- "Although she's not as stacked as her bridesmaids. . . ."
- "During shock therapy, I really learned a lot about commitment."
- "Here's to *my* future filled with *her* home-cooked meals."
- "Love is a mysterious thing. It's like a mass murderer who sneaks up behind you with one of those steel strings that can slice through your flesh like butter."
- ". . . and she understands, how can I put this, a man's feminine side."
- "To the first girl I've ever met who didn't hesitate to sign the prenuptials."
- "I mean, her photos were the talk of the gym's locker room."
- "I think I'm gonna throw up."

8:00 PM—Dancing, dancing, talking, seeing food served, filming, dancing, drinking, watching people eat, dancing, talking, kissing, dancing, drinking, watching people eat, talking, thanking, dancing, talking, filming, dancing, drinking, watching people eat, dancing, talking, kissing, dancing, drinking, talking, thanking, seeing plates removed, dancing, kissing, cake cutting, dancing, good-bye mumbling, drinking, dancing.

11:59:59 PM—Band packs up in the middle of Kool and the Gang medley.

12:28 AM—Tearful embraces.

12:54 AM—Arrive at a site with a bed.

YOUR WIFE: You're drunk.

YOU: No, I'm snot. C'meer, you little filly.

YOUR WIFE: You had to prove to all your buddies you were a man tonight or something?

YOU: I sorry sweetness, c'meer and let me show you what a man I am.

YOUR WIFE: I married a drunk.

YOU: And Mr. Happy would like to toast the newlyweds.

YOUR WIFE: Don't touch me!

YOU: Great.

YOUR WIFE: Great. You're sleeping on the floor.

YOU: This is perfect. This is just like my dad said marriage would be.

1:00 AM—Make passionate married love.

1:03 AM—Roll over.

1:04 AM—Regroup and cuddle.

Through your haze, you remember that turning your back on your wife after having sex is a horrible thing to do. Either that or she dug her nails into your back. Hopefully you will force yourself to embrace her. She will probably want to relive the wedding. You'll laugh, you'll cry. It'll be the feel good night of the summer.

Take a good look at your beautiful bride and remind yourself to stuff any lingering resentment deep, deep inside. Caress her and talk into the wee hours. Just don't allow any of the following thoughts to be sent out by your overworked cranial lobes.

What Not to Say in Bed on Your Wedding Night

- "Is this wedding cake I feel?"
- "I wonder who was on Letterman?"
- "I really can't stay the whole night, I've got an early meeting."
- "All that ''til death do us part' stuff's got Mr. Happy in a funk."

- "Hold that thought, I've got to call my bookie."
- "Damn it, and here I was told it would get better after we took our vows."
- "The other wives should be here any minute."
- "Get down on all fours and let me give you a mammoth screwing like the one I took on your engagement ring."
- "Are you through yet?"
- "Go grab me a cold one."
- "Just think, you can have two minutes like that any night you want, for the rest of your life."
- "Hey, you're on my side of the bed again."

1:05 AM—Contemplate the end of your life.
4:32 AM—Wake from lack of oxygen, remind heart to stop skipping beats.

Chapter Four

Honeymooning and Beyond

The Seven-Year Bitch

The Honeymoon

You awaken the morning after your wedding calm, blissful, and serene. You get a glimpse of your new wife asleep and you think this could be the happiest moment of your life. She rolls over and, in the cutest voice your ears have ever heard, says, "I think it's adorable the way you have kept the honeymoon plans a secret. So, honey, where are you whisking me?"

Honeymoon? Plans? You start to think back over the advice you have read in this book. You don't remember any honeymoon planning section. Did you read the fine print? Do you recall the part where it says, "The authors are not responsible in any way for the outcome (unless positive) of any wedding, relationship, or life"? "Damn them, damn them all to hell," you think. "They didn't warn me about this honeymoon thing."

Have no fear, if you really forgot to think of the honeymoon, then the woman who married you is probably gullible enough to be satisfied with our "Honeymoon at Home"™ suggestions. But don't count on it. Pick up the phone, with your credit card in hand, and start to hustle your way out of the country.

Honeymoon at Home™

She Wants To	You Need To
See ancient ruins	Invite over eighty-year-old nudists
Play water sports	Cross streams in the shower
Expose herself to new people	Throw open the curtains when she's changing
Hobnob with great culinary geniuses of Europe	Introduce her to Chef Boyardee
Enjoy complete solitude	Lock her in the closet
Stay at a bed and breakfast	Have loud neighbors share your bathroom, tie up your phone, and babble during meals
Learn about foreign cultures	Keep the yogurt out for a week
Sleep under the stars	Smack her over the head at bedtime
Eat dinner over the water and under the moon	Serve her a sandwich in the tub and pull down your pants

Congratulations. You figured out how to book a plane flight and are sitting on an exotic beach picking your teeth with a tiny parasol. Now you figure you can let your guard down, be yourself again, and finally unwind. Guess again, Chester. Your new wife has an agenda for this little vacation that you know nothing about. She has accumulated a mental list of sunrise-to-sunset, hand-holding, bicycle-built-for-two excursions that is as long as your upcoming mini-bar tab. In fact, the way in which you react to each of her "ideas" will be your first major test as a married man. That's right, say it out loud, "married man." There will be endless other tests, but since this is your first, it counts extra. Your wife wants to see how you act away from all the courting, planning, and partying. This is where the rule book of the rest of your life is being written. Keep your guard high and don't say any of the following, no matter how sunbaked you get.

Things Not to Find Yourself Saying
on Your Honeymoon

- "Don't you wish my parents were here?"
- "I had no idea a seat cushion could float so well."
- "Like these sunsets are any different from the ones we get back home."
- "The brochure didn't mention anything about riots and the ritualistic slaying of all foreigners."
- "How do you say remote control in Italian?"
- "Geez, I remember Uncle Phil's trailer being a lot roomier."
- "Honey, can you put away those thighs? I can't read the sports page with all that light bouncing into my eyes."
- "Well, we've never seen a tidal wave with the destructive force of a hydrogen bomb lay waste to beachfront property together."

- "Oh, great, this place's got reruns of *Three's Company.*"
- "No, really. It's just a coincidence that all my groomsmen have rooms right next to ours."
- "No, Mr. Malden, they weren't American Express."
- "Do you think I should help that poor girl put some sun-tan lotion on those nipples?"
- "You said Paris. You said absolutely nothing about France."
- "*Cerveza* for everyone, on us?"
- "Oh my God, look at that guy parasailing in a Speedo. I think it's my bookie."
- "What was that whole deal about a seven-day itch?"
- "It's not like this is a once in a lifetime experience."

Moving In

For your sake, we hope you didn't think the hassles would all be over after the ceremony and the honeymoon. The only thing that's over is your former freewheeling lifestyle. For the wedding you had to learn a couple of terms, nod a lot, and show up with your fly zipped.

For post-wedding life you will actually have to change your ways. You will have to sleep on the wall side of the bed. You will have to shower. You will have to speak to another human being before you have had a cup of coffee in the morning. And (you might want to sit down for this) after you've had sex, no matter how many times you tell her that you really have to get to work early in the morning, she will not leave. To make this shocking situation easier to swallow for you, we have devised a list of utterances that should never be voiced during the acclimation period.

Things Not to Mention While Moving in Together

- "When the television's on, you cease to exist, okay?"
- "You can keep your sweaters under the bed, and only under the bed, right next to my porno mags."
- "I know the toilet seat's always up. Ever heard the word *squat?*"
- "Touch my stereo and you'll wish you hadn't."
- "If you'd drop a few, this place would feel much more spacious."
- "When your parents come to stay with us, they get the floor."
- "Fetch!"
- "And my Women of the Big Ten calendar can go right here."
- "I looked it up in a book, and wet towels do indeed belong on the back of a wooden chair."
- "What are you doing out of the kitchen?"
- "So I used your face cream to grease my bicycle chain. Are you going to make a federal case out of it?"
- "From now on, I shall call you 'Mom.'"
- "I took the liberty of throwing out some of your 'extra' shoes."
- "Every Thursday is *Deliverance* night, got that?"
- "Love me . . . love my stink."
- "You sleep on my side of the bed for more than a minute and you can kiss this little thing called marriage good-bye."

The Old Ways

You are beginning to settle into married life. It's not too bad. You go home with a beautiful woman every night, and you aren't even drunk half the time. The wedding pictures have been sorted and put into an album, and you've only chipped one piece of crystal.

Yet there are certain parts of your old life that you miss — the smell of laundry festering under your bed, the sodium-enhanced flavor of a warm Hungry Man dinner, the caramel tint your walls used to get when you ate the worm out of the bottom of a tequila bottle. Some of the charms of single life can still be found in your new freedomless existence. Only now, for each old habit tasted, there is a sour price to pay.

Trade in America

You Want To	You Will Have To
Hang out with the boys one night a week	Hang out with her mother one day a weekend
Smoke cigars in the house	Forget you know what kissing is
Have peace and quiet	Physically remove both your eardrums
Watch nonstop football in winter, baseball in summer	Make hell freeze over
Burp whenever the feeling strikes	Grimace whenever she strikes
Keep your *Playboy* collection	Hide them thoroughly
Stay in contact with old girlfriends	Occasionally remove the kitchen knife from your back
Eat your meals in front of the TV	Eat your meals with a straw
Keep your old comfy sofa	Sleep on it

The Negotiations

As statistical studies have proven, there are three main sources of marital grief—the logistical struggles over the remote control, the toilet seat, and the garbage container. Of course, excluded from the study was money, sex, familial infighting, housing situations, child rearing, schooling, career frustration, and about forty other areas that we're too lazy to input into the computer. Suffice it to say that the three included in this book are the most critical.

The study revealed that as tension mounts in each area, it is incumbent upon the husband to exert firmness in his dealings with his wife and the problematic situation. That's right, offer a hearty "No problem, Sweetie" and hustle to your appointed task. Then, when she isn't around, contemplate quick implementation of the following ploys.

The Remote Control

This little baby has broken up more marriages than Sharon Stone. First, realize that men and women both use the remote like they're dating. No matter what a man is watching, he always suspects there may be something better on the next channel. Once a woman finds a show she likes, she will see the show through its highs and lows, try to communicate with the show, maybe even talk about the relationship. TACK TO TAKE: Learn to palm an AA battery like a magician. When your wife gets tired of the remote going on the blink when she uses it, the apparatus will return to its rightful position in the middle of your meaty palm.

The Toilet Seat

Men don't really understand the woman's basic argument here. Has a woman ever really fallen in? Yet that's what they claim with deadly seriousness. There is no arguing on this one. TACK TO TAKE: To train your wife that leaving the seat up is not much of a crime, begin to close the seat but leave worse things on the rim. A cold splash of water will pale in comparison to a piece of chewed food or thumbtack or one of those gummy candy worms.

The Garbage

Female logic dictates: You see it, you take it out. And although many men have come into marriage with enlightened ideas like "chore sharing," equal rights end where decomposition begins. (This would include performing autopsies, rummaging through dump sites, and unraveling piano concertos.) TACK TO TAKE: Convince your wife that taking out the trash is a fun family game, like Jenga. The last person to stack a piece of refuse in the garbage can before the pile tips over is the winner. The loser takes it out. It's that simple.

The Single Ones

You're living in marital bliss, still flush with wedding excitement and that bout of dysentery you contracted on the honeymoon. You are going back into the world a happily married man with a tan and your friends sense the difference. Everywhere that you and your wife go, you run into single acquaintances who cast jealous leers in your direction. Before you go off, keep in mind that it wasn't long ago that you were rubbing up against anything that wasn't a bar stool, attempting to find happiness in the dismal world of single living. Before you shoot one of the following arrows of haughty happiness into the backs of lonely souls, try to remember how you used to feel.

Things Not to Say to Jealous Friends or Relatives

- "Don't worry, you'll get hitched someday . . . to a post, whenever you go horseback riding."
- "I know you'll always have to take my word for it, but love is a really incredible thing."
- "Have you ever considered adoption? That single-parent thing is big nowadays."
- "Try to find solace in the truth of that old adage, 'You're born alone, you die alone.'"
- "Here's a photo of us so you won't forget what we look like now that we're married."
- "I've heard cats make great companions."
- "Don't you hate the gods for making you, you."
- "At least you have virtual reality to look forward to."

- "When I said I'll always be there for you, I hope you real-ize it was in the figurative sense."
- "Think of all the money you save by not having anyone to buy gifts for on the holidays."
- "I'm actually envious of all the time you have to read at night."
- "I can remember when, just like you, I couldn't find a healthy relationship if it was biting my nuts off."
- "Try not to feel like you're being left behind. Of course you are, just try not to feel like that."
- "We're so fortunate to know someone like you. Because we'll always have someone free to baby-sit when we need it."

Fight Break

FIGHT TOPIC: THE GARAGE SALE

YOUR WIFE: If you don't sell them, I will.

YOU: Fine. Then I'm keeping my collection of *Rear View* magazine.

YOUR WIFE: Over my dead body.

YOU: Have it your way. Do you want to be drowned, poisoned, or stabbed?

YOUR WIFE: I'm sacrificing a lot here, so we can start fresh. You've got to get rid of some of your crap.

YOU: I am, dammit.

YOUR WIFE: I don't think a stack of yellowing undies with tattered waistbands really counts.

YOU: They're still a hell of a lot more supportive than you are.

YOUR WIFE: So Mr. Sass-mouth, that's why I'm selling all my furniture and you're not. That's why I'm getting rid of most of my childhood mementos so our new home, our new life together, can be free of clutter.

YOU: If you were really committed to that, we'd sell your sister out on the lawn Saturday.

YOUR WIFE: That's all you have to add?

YOU: Don't get mad. She'd probably fetch forty bucks or so.

YOUR WIFE: Great. Keep your underpants and your old clothes and your coasters-from-around-the-world collec-

tion. But we're spending our meager profits on kitchen utensils.

YOU: Did you get this torture training from the army or something?

YOUR WIFE: Fair is fair.

YOU: You win. I'll sell my underwear. But I'm not going to give it away. Rest assured of that.

Shopping for a Home

You've started getting used to the m-word and are beginning to believe that buying a house together will be a process in which you are actually involved. Picturing an actual house might seem exhilarating—a big-screen TV in the living room, an extra Frigidaire just for beer, maybe even mirrors on the bedroom ceiling. Yeah, that's right, you will be the king of some snazzy royal digs on top of a lush, green. . . . Sorry, but it's time to wake from that nap. You won't be the ruler of anything. If you are lucky, you'll be friends with the court jester.

In fact, the sooner you take those dreams of king and castle and exchange them for kitchen wallpaper and a toilet brush, the easier life will be for you. Plan on spending most of your weekends hitting the streets with the local real estate pages and an incapacitating migraine. With all of your wife's impossible criteria, you'll be running in circles faster than someone with one foot nailed to the floor and a belly full of high-fiber supplements. Don't compound your hassles by asking any of these questions when you two are out looking for that new love nest.

Questions Not to Ask the Realtor

- "Is it close to a topless bar?"
- "Does it have a room that will hold like, let's say, ten guys and a pool table?"
- "Are any of the neighbors cute?"
- "Wait a minute here, I agreed to the marriage thing, but who said anything about living together?"
- "Does the place come with a lot of stuff strewn everywhere, or is that extra?"
- "Why would my wife want central heating when she's got my hairy ass to keep her warm in winter?"
- "Is the roof strong enough to hold a couple of satellite dishes?"
- "Will the bank accept vintage *Playboys* as collateral?"
- "Are the walls thick? Because we need 'em thick, if you know what I mean."
- "Can you show us something built over an Indian burial ground?"
- "Is the place near a bus stop? Some of my other wives don't drive."
- "What would we want with a termite inspection?"
- "Escrow, schmescrow. Can I see the size of the crapper?"
- "Is this area zoned for cock fighting?"
- "How much?"

The Writing of a Will

You really should start giving some thought to writing your thank-you notes. But since you're looking for things to keep you busy in the meantime, aside from watching the woman next door sponge bathe and counting the divots in a golf ball, we recommend working up a draft of a last will and testament. You are married now and hopefully have a tidy treasure trove of valuables. It would be a shame to see your goodies go to probate lawyers in the event that you expire, let's say, at the hands of an angry neighbor.

I, (*fill in your name*), being of strong mind and bladder, do hereby bequeath the following items. To my loving, devoted wife, I leave you my balls, which you actually busted early in our relationship. If they prove salvageable, consider giving them to your father. He certainly needs a good set. I also leave you what's left of our savings that I haven't spent on drink and prostitutes. The car, which I assume you'll drive every week to my cemetery plot, should be taken to a mechanic soon. I'd been spending that money at the track. My best guess is that the car hasn't had a tune-up in about six years. My parents, if they're still with us, lost the one thing they ever cared for when you made me slap that diamond ring on your finger, so nothing I leave them can ever make up for that. Oh, speaking of your ring, I think you'll probably need to pawn it as soon as possible to hold off the creditors. Maybe you could use the cash to move to Canada and start a new life there. I wish you all the best, my love. See you in the next life . . . well, not too soon I hope. I need a little time to myself. You understand.

The Thank-You Notes

There are strict rules about writing thank-you notes. As guys, however, we don't happen to be familiar with any of them. What we do know is that the modern woman is not solely responsible for thanking all your guests for their meager contributions to your life. Generally, the groom gets the thrill of writing to his side of the guest list.

The best way to combat the frustration of thinking of unique expressions of gratitude is to develop a template—a basic form letter, in which you plug in the gift and name particulars. When constructing your note, honesty is strictly off-limits. Unless you got cash back on a specific gift item, there isn't going to be a hell of a lot of thanks to go around.

This lack of forthrightness will, we're sure, conflict with everything you stand for as a human being. Put a lid on your integrity and line up the mistruths. If the gift was horrendous, probably recycled from the giver's own wedding sometime during the Carter administration, use the word "generous." If you hate the guests' guts, having invited them out of obligation or because they gave birth to you, thank them "for making your special day all the more special." Get it? Well, just make sure you never implement any portion of a thank-you note like this. . . .

Dear $250-a-head,

I hope you enjoyed drinking more than your share of our top-shelf alcohol. We enjoyed giving you a cursory hug and then ignoring you for the rest of the party. We are not sure exactly at this point why you were on the final list, but your spastic dance moves will keep us in stitches for years as we watch the video with people we really care about. Thank you so much for the wineglasses or place setting or juicer or talking scale or crystal farm animal or velvet Elvis print or other. Your thoughtfulness was really touching. We'll always think of you when we see a twenty spot.

Last Call

A Conclusion

There you have it. This book is finished, and you're well on your way to old age and all the aches 'n' pains that come with it. You've made it through the biggest day of *her* life. For your sake, try not to push the wedding memories too deeply into the outer recesses of your atrophying mind. Someday soon there just might be a little voice asking you all about the time you got married.

No, it won't be your invisible pal Billy looking to get back in your good graces after that naked-shadow-puppet debacle. It will be a son or a daughter asking those peculiar questions that only kids do. No, not "why do I have to pull your finger?" It will be much more powerful than even that. You'll be slurping down a beer or driving across town, or both, when suddenly your offspring will say something like, "Daddy, if you had to do it all over again, would you marry Mommy?"

"Yes," you'll tell your child without hesitation, as surprising as that sounds, "I would marry Mom again. She's the greatest woman in the world and our wedding was the biggest, most incredible day of *my* life. In fact, I'd give one of my recently nonfunctional body parts to live it all over again—the planning, the shopping, the fisticuffs with your grandma—every last glorious detail."

So then, keep the memories fresh. Fight safely. Remain faithful and enjoy each other. Staying married is much like attaining public office. It's all about fraud. But that's another book altogether. Good luck.

Thesaurus of Related Terminology

Baseball (n): sporting event, the national pastime, a summertime treat in which you arrive in the third inning and are forced to leave in the fifth.

Bedroom (n): sleeping quarters, dream closet, actionless house space.

Caterer (n): chef, food server, that no-good #%@#-*%*#@&*%^*!!!

Dishwashing (n): cleaning the plates, scrubbing the utensils, "your damn turn."

Divorce (v): to split up, to dissolve, to give her ½, the lawyer ¼, the shrink ⅒, the bartender 1/20, your bookie 1/20, and various dating services whatever's left.

Effort (n): exertion, output, what you're not giving enough of and don't even care.

Girlfriend (n): a female companion, a pal that is a woman; it don't matter what she is, she ain't never coming over.

Heartburn (n): reflux, pyrosis, your new best buddy.

In-Laws, HERS (n): your parents, your folks, your family that is never right and always a bother.

In-Laws, YOURS (n): her parents, her folks, her well-behaved, never out-of-line, always-welcomed-to-tag-along loved ones.

Leisure (n): freedom, relaxation, what only single guys have.

Marry (v): to wed, to unite in holy bliss (female connotation), to castrate in ancient unnecessary ritual (male connotation).

Ogle (v): to leer, to eye lecherously, to enjoy the one remaining pleasure in your control.

Opinion (n): belief, view, the bride's judgment, which is all that matters in situations of importance.

Ordinary (adj): basic, plain, the worst comment known to womankind.

Orifice (n): opening, hole, that of which you will be given an extra if you arrive late to any arranged appointment.

Paycheck (n): Needed income, hard-earned monies, female shopping enhancer.

Plant Watering (n): feeding the foliage, drenching the greenery, "your damn responsibility."

Positively-Absolutely (adv): certainly-definitely, without question, the only acceptable response to the question, "Do you like these things my mom and I just picked out?"

Rain (n): precipitation, showers, the enemy of all that is holy which, contrary to Alanis Morissette, is not ironic . . . it is generally histrionic.

Sex (n): intercourse, lovemaking, a privilege or a chore (always alternating).

Toilet-Fixing (n): potty plunging, crapper correcting, "your damn job."

Wife (n): spouse, betrothed, life partner, the love of your life, the exalted one, the lawmaker, the winner of every argument, the ruler of the roost, the owner of your soul, the controller of your will to live, the queen, the maker of plans with her friends, the breaker of plans with yours, the judge and the jury, the only non-blood-related woman who loves you unconditionally for who you are.